Sixty
Odd

Sixty Odd

New Poems

URSULA K. LE GUIN

SHAMBHALA

Boston & London

1999

Shambhala Publications, Inc.
Horticultural Hall
300 Massachusetts Avenue
Boston, MA 02115
http://www.shambhala.com

9   8   7   6   5   4   3   2   1

First Edition

Printed in the United States of America

⊛ This edition is printed on acid-free paper that meets the
American National Standards Institute Z39.48 Standard.

Distributed in the United States by Random House, Inc.,
and in Canada by Random House of Canada Ltd

Library of Congress Cataloging-in-Publication Data
Le Guin, Ursula K., 1929–
    Sixty odd: new poems/by Ursula K. Le Guin.—1st ed.
    p. cm.
    Includes index.
    ISBN 1–57062–388–0 (pbk.: alk. paper)
    I. Title.
PS3562.E42S5   1999   98–37084
811'.54—dc21   CIP

Contents

Preface

I've been introduced to people who said to me, with what looked like a delicious shudder of vanity, "Oh, I'm so afraid you'll put me in your next novel!"

I say, "Don't worry, I never do that," which is true; it would be cruel to say, "Don't worry, I have to compost you first." But that would be the honest answer from any writer who aspires to more than journalism (or revenge). Fiction is an imaginative art. Characters in a novel aren't reproductions, they're inventions. To invent them, novelists draw not just on their acquaintance with one person or another but on their life experience of other people and their own self-knowledge.

I do sometimes realize that I stole a character's ears from Dr. Oppenheimer, or that another snaps her handbag the way a friend of mine does, but I recognize such a trait-theft with dismay, like a melon seed that survived the compost and comes sprouting up among the pansies.

But that's fiction. What about poetry?

It seems to me that the connection of poetry with experience is more immediate and intense than that of prose, yet more oblique and mysterious—altogether more paradoxical. And that our poetry is often less inventive, more literal, than our fiction.

My poems begin in two ways (that I am aware of), which I think of as "catching" and "following." One is a desire to catch, hold, surround, describe the sight, the emotion, the vision, a passionate desire that forces the words into poetry. A longing to take hold, a longing to make sense.

Or the words begin to make a rhythm, or grow out of a rhythm, coming of themselves and following their own logic, and lead the writing hand and the writer's mind to follow them—halting or racing, amazed or bewildered—wherever they go. If they make sense, it comes as a gift, a discovery.

"Catching" usually involves description, representation, and may involve or imply story—and portraiture. "Following" works by metaphor and without narrative. In the process of writing and rewriting, of course the two processes are likely to combine; maybe in origin they are the same.

There are poems of both kinds in the first part of this book, "Circling to Descend."

In the second part, all the poems started with the longing to "catch," to hold or understand. For a few months I was impelled to write about people I had known: not in fiction, nor yet biographically, but in poetry, and therefore in some sense autobiographically. I wanted the poems to re-present what these people had been *to me*. I wanted to reach back to them, to circle back, uniting now with then, here with there, self with other, a round dance I think many of us dance in our minds as we grow old. Finding these people again, I felt I was catching glimpses of myself through them. That's why I call this gallery of portraits "The Mirror Gallery."

What I wrote was autobiographical but certainly not an autobiography. I couldn't choose the subjects. The memories were as self-willed as the words. I wasn't in charge. I couldn't even follow, but only wait. Only those who wished to come would come, and most of them were the dead. Some of my people wouldn't show me their face, but wore a mask; for these, and those still alive, I used invented names. Some people I hadn't thought of for years came to join this round dance, while some I loved most did not. My father and brothers are scarcely mentioned, my husband and children not at all. The selection from the past is partial, following a way of its own towards a discovery that remains obscure. Getting older, we're likely to get used to following paths in the dark.

Part One

CIRCLING TO DESCEND

Start Here

I begin again at sixty-one.

Nobody ever said
this word before
this word after
this word
this way.
Nobody ever.

But only isn't always honest,
nor first truest.
What shall I trust?

Begin again.
Start here.
This word.

I try to be true.
I lie and I
begin again.

Must I trust
you?

Hexagram 45

Gather round me all my words!
Aunty Change has said to gather,
said the Emperor comes to the palace.
Come closer to me, closer!
Arrange yourselves in order,
peasants, merchants, artisans, lords,
common nouns and working verbs,
beautiful adjectives, names of glory.
Assume your syntax, raise your swords,
shouting, roaring, inventing meanings.
Save me from the silent demons.
Where there's blue shout red! red!
Where there's end make story, story.

Dreamwordplay

Fishes swallow ashes of hashish.
The mind's wishes follow shadows
down hollows to the owl's places,
find bones of mouse and vole and shrew
in owl's feces small and whole,
fishbones in the mouse's hole.
Flashing swallows with human faces
float down now as ashes, ashes.

A Circle in a Drought

Somewhere in this country
of dry furrow and hard hill
the scabbed ground cracks
to a deep blade of shining,
a bright upwelling,
mud, rush, mess, hurry of voices,
the run, the flood, the telling.

I walk forward, careful.
The forked switch leads me.
Surely it will dip, leap
there at the end of the field
where dead stalks rub each other,
or there in the dry creekbed
where rocks tell the tale of torrent.

I must learn to live drily.
What to carry. What to leave.
What to drink instead of water.
What to wash the dust away with.
What to listen to. Wind
will tell me what to say.
Stone will lead me to beginning.

Redescending

He who turned upon her sings
striking his lyre, the lover
sweeter than ever.
      Beasts go about their business,
trees are indifferent,
rocks hard as any heart.
Only the women in the bushes,
wild girls, hair unbraided,
listen, peering from cover.
As he sobs in the melodic
climax of his art,
they grunt and snigger
with anger, they come at him
loose-chapped as lionesses.
      He is rent from the center,
gutted, dismembered.
      The head floats,
mouth open on a high note.
      Bearing the lyre the river
runs to the entrance and falls.

Down in the silence
Euridice gathers him.
By Lethe she pieces him,
on those dark margins,
the sands of remembrance.
      Holding the hollow
lyre unstrung, and dumb,
he faces her once more.
"This time follow me,"

she says, and he follows.
She does not look back.

A long way in silence
by the dry sea with one shore,
a long way without turning
to the place of returning.
       There she can turn to him
at last, and he into her: there
the curved hand strikes the doubled chord
and other is no longer: there
are interpenetrations of bodies
of words, fecund, there
under the roots of the hair of the mothers
in the realm of the maidens
where the unborn surrounds
the womb, and the fathers
dream in the curled
hands of the child who comes to be
in the world, braiding
and twining vibrations
rejoining and voices
rejoined.

When there aren't any

and when nothing beats,
no crow just past the edge of sight
heavily seeking, no echo dogging
the syllable, no rim of light
around the sound, no feet
dancing, what do you do?

Suck the mud and wait.

Mudsucker mudsucker seeking to say
what? say what? is it right
to say what's left to say? whose right?

O I have earned my urn, and sixty years
of spading at my grave has dug it hole enough
for all my little partialities.

World,
you interpenetrate my mesh. The tendriled gods
still climb my spine, stars are my tears,
birds wing my feet and lions lick my hair,
but the net of mankind wears so thin
that the old soul falls through, slick fish,
cynic butterfly, shadow of a crow.
What shall I say in the speech
that tears the web to shreds,
the tongue of my killing people?
Can singing heal the sea?

I will suck sand, talk salt.
I will fear silence. Grandmother!
Teach me the weaving
and the words to be said.

Rodmell

When we walked in the garden of love
lovers were walking there
alone, in couples, in threes
under the apple trees in the uncertain air.

Nobody was there but lovers,
silently seeking what they wanted:
the river where she set down her burden
near the garden he planted.

Wind washes over the long light downs.
By her house walk those who love her.
She became the river and was burned to ashes
and there is no earth above her.

Read at the Award Dinner, May 1996

Beware when you honor an artist.
You are praising danger.
You are holding out your hand
to the dead and the unborn.
You are counting on what cannot be counted.

The poet's measures serve anarchic joy.
The story-teller tells one story: freedom.

Above all beware of honoring women artists.
For the housewife will fill the house with lions
and in with the grandmother
come bears, wild horses, great horned owls, coyotes.

For Gabriela Mistral

En el Valle de Elqui, ceñido
de cien montañas o de mas . . .

Forty years beyond her mortal years
she came back to me, to our Pacific,
she came here, she
who sank the meek and blinded saint
and the grim men from Spain
in the glory of the lord of angels
and a gust of the craziest wind.
She stood on his northern shore
where gulls whirled like torn paper
and said in the language that I spoke
before I spoke words, "Come!"

"Come!" she said, standing
heavy-bodied and rough-voiced,
deep-breasted as the hills:
"I came north, but you didn't know me.
I've gone home now to the valley
encircled by a hundred mountains,
a hundred mountains, maybe more.
You must come and you must learn
my language."

                    If I walk south
with the ocean always on my right
and the mountains on my left,
swimming the mouths of the rivers,
the estuaries and the great canal,
if I walk from high tide to low tide

and full moon to new moon, south,
and from equinox to solstice, south,
across the equator in a dream of volcanoes,
if I walk through all the Tropics
past bays of amethyst and bays of jade
from April spring to April autumn, south,
and cross the deserts of niter and asbestos
with the sea silver on my right
and a hundred mountains on my left,
a hundred mountains, maybe more,
I will come to the valley.

If I walk all the way, my poet,
if I can walk all the way,
I will come to you.
And I will speak your language.

Hexagram 49

How could I not love her? She
wants what cannot be
owned, or known, or gone;
the way she seeks to find
is the other one; the me
she hunts does not exist, her
"baby, mother, friend, sister,"
purer, stronger than ever I
or woman was, her "interlocutor
in the secret rivers of the mind."

She transforms all to forest.
She shames the owning, knowing,
gaining of an end, she shines
incandescent, without compromise.
All that was and will be lost
is golden in the puma's eyes.

The fire in the secret river.
How could I not love her?

Four Morning Poems

1. Elisabeth Making Candied Rose Petals, 1972

Early morning early summer
and the singing from garden to garden,
sprays, borders, light and laden,
lithe-blossoming, in mortal danger,
unguarded, brief, one day, one morning,

yet see, reborn
past all changes,
chances, closes,
bright beyond danger,
the rose among roses.

2. The Uses of Morning

I

The uses of morning are holy.

It wells up clear from sleep
so the soul can drink, crouching,
hands on cold moss and mud,
unprotected from the hunter
and bearing the dream in her belly.

___

What do you do with the sun
before it rises?

Let it show you ways hidden
by the thickets of light.

Look for it over curving bows
down in the broken water of darkness
falling away, falling away behind.

Wait for it. Wait for the lion
to come. Patiently wait for the hunter
to come to the summons.

3. *Morning Service*

So still so sunny and so Sunday
is this early day,
what's done needs to be silent:
a white butterfly
by the red fuses of the fuchsias.

The sounds are the sea
that only breaks its silence
meeting other elements,
and a hummingbird saying tek!
tek! as it attacks the fuchsias.

Nothing else says anything.
I am trying to be still.
This is the church I go to
to hear the hymns and prayers
and see the light.

4. *Bird at Dawn, February*

In the deep ogive of the dawn
freshness, to hold still
and so be given this first voice
so far, so early in the dark
that will be spring, that will
again and still be all
tendril, freshet, frond unfolding, song
again and still again and still.

Late Dusk

The sky is rose quartz amethyst
over dark hill dark trees dark roof.
Say dark so long it has no meaning.
Say I would be farther west.
Say I am not far enough.
Say the light is beautiful, failing.

Fall

O No
vember
held gold
past ember
last flash
kestrel over
amber red gash rust
to bare
endure and somber
clear
yes

January 7

The black king whose lifted arm ends
at the wrist goes in
with the cross donkey,
the uncomprehending ox,
and the shepherd boy whose flute tweedles
silently to staring German camels.
I gather soft palm branches together
again into the dark of the year.
Even the tissue paper is seventy years old
and we're on the third Jesus.

By the Canal

Ducks are passing pair by pair,
one in water one in air:

breast almost to breast they fly,
each bearing its own image by.

One below and one above,
untouching and untouched they move.

Flight 1067 to L.A.

Snowy sierra sawteeth
lift to leftward
as I drink white wine staidly
above the Great Valley in the belly
of a silvery pseudocetacean
sailing the airsea to a palmy city.
I am my ancestors' sci-fi.

Malheur Maar

A hole in black ground.
Steep cliff walls round.
A ring of tall green reeds
under the walls around the water.
Some small people sit here and there silently
on the cliffs among rabbitbrush and sagebrush.
Some small people silently
climb up my pants leg.
In the round water
are the reeds and the walls
and some of the people
and the wind moving
and the silence.

Acorn Woodpecker

When I've been dead a hundred years
down in the dust, adobe in my ears,
if I hear that laugh and purr
my soul will put on a red clown head
and crazy wings and fly with her.

III

Infinitive

We make too much history.

With or without us
there will be the silence
and the rocks and the far shining.

But what we need to be
is, oh, the small talk of swallows
in evening over
dull water under willows.

To be we need to know the river
holds the salmon and the ocean
holds the whales as lightly
as the body holds the soul
in the present tense, in the present tense.

"The scarcity of rhinos" on the television

"The scarcity of rhinos"
(unimaginably)
"in this region
is such that individuals
only are known."
They run from the camera. The scarcity
of imagination, the paucity
of rhinos, the poverty
of cities, the scarcity
of probity, are probably
connected.
The rhinos of invention
are poorer than the individuals
in the cities of the poverty
of the imagination of the politicians
of paucity.

O rhinoceroses of unimaginable real horns
of plenty on savannahs of enormous
vegetables and animals and connections!

Individuals make moving pictures
of the extinction of 300 species
daily and individually
watch them running
into the distances
of all the plenty
of the indivisible world.

The horn of the rhinoceros
finely divided is imagined

to assure longevity
to the human
individual.

O awkward and shortsighted
and short-lived rhinoceros,
bearing the living
horn, the one true one!
Where?

On 23rd Street

She looked at me clearly
eye into eye and said clearly
as if across a dining table,
"You see, my parents never told me
it was the Communists."
She wore a soiled hot-pink leotard
and many other clothes, and other
clothes and other things
were in her wire cart. She went on
talking as I went on past,
explaining why she was angry.
I could not understand and only thought,
O Lord, if I was her mother
and saw her like this!
I am her mother and I see her
like this.

Appropriation

Is it appropriate that a woman mourn
a bird?
            A fledgling acorn woodpecker, in
a hole in the old elm over the picnic table:
all week we watched the adults come and feed it.
Heard it fizzing and wheedling, learning to purr,
louder every day. Took a picture
of the small, alert, black-white-and-red
head looking out. Yelled and threw stones
at the Steller's jay that came to kill it shrieking.
Winged the jay, but didn't save the fledgling.
So that's the story.
            The parents, relatives,
the little tribe that had looked after it,
never came back to the elm. They stayed
up in the oaks, up on the knoll, flashes
of black-white-red, the dipping flight,
calling and purring, many conversations.
Birds don't mourn.
            How can a human being
cry for a bird in a world where children
suffer in terror? Species die daily.
Men bomb undefended cities.
Torture. Prison camps. Dead forests.
A world of enormous sorrows.
It is out of all proportion.
            I mourn
in my proportion, for one death, not wrong,
not out of nature, a life-sized death.
My grief, sharp as a knife the first night,

is dull, small, long. Aching for words.
      So I name this death, as birds do not,
and women do, appropriate it,
make it my own: the little one that had
no chance to fly.

FIELD BURNING DEBATED.
SALMON FATE DISCUSSED.

We are the desert god.
His left hand plucks from the burning
what his right hand burns.

The farmer in the photo holds a stalk of fescue:
"To you people it's just grass.
To me it's money."
In autumn it goes up in smoke,
a fitting sacrifice.

The nations of the salmon
return upriver to the festival
of the nations of the desert,
leap, and become money in midair.
There is no festival.

The god debates fate
while with his hands he feeds his mouth
and eats the fingers one by one.

October 11, 1491

In a year and a day
they will be here.
     Do not go down to the seashore!
     Hide the food, the ornaments,
     hide with the children in the mountains!
In a year and a day
the wizards will arrive.
     Do not go forward to them!
     Give them nothing!
You will see three ships come sailing in.
Out of the east the kings will come.
And the world will grow old
that morning. It will begin to die
for the first time. It will die
of the sickness of pustules,
the sickness of coughing,
the sickness of money,
the sickness of landowning,
the sickness of the old god
of the old world, the rich people.

The young world,
the red clay world
of puma, jaguar, buffalo,
of hummingbird, gourd, and sequoia,
of corn, vicuña, sacred tobacco,
the center of the six directions,
the dawn-smelling world, the fern-stem world,
will live for a year and a day.

Then you will go forward with your empty hands,
timid and smiling, and give it to them.

Lost Arrows and The Feather People

Small claws of an acorn woodpecker
in the roofpeak over my head:
squawks and purring, "wackawacka!"
exploratory taps
on the housewall.

If it, if they're right, is war,
life a battle, every kitchen
Iwo Jima and the bed Thermopylae,
then we have to be warriors, winners
or else won, prizes, Sabines slung
like quarters of mutton behind the heroes.
We have to be armed.
Every kid his Colt, his .22,
machine guns for grown-ups,
bombs for the real biggies,
the boss men, los Generales.
All chiefs. No injuns.

The mourning dove
calls in the digger pines
across the creek
across the rainy air.

Why do I keep thinking
you can, if you just know how,
and it takes luck too, what doesn't?—choose—
instead of being drafted or enlisting
and bearing arms in defense of got and cunt
and los Generales—choose to be
not a hero. To be

something else. What else?
A deserter?

>Sun has gleamed out.
>A silent wind
>stirs wet branches.
>From the big oak's new lime-green
>leaves, soft-lobed,
>drops bright water.

A hippie? A victim?
Somebody there isn't any use for.
A civilian?

>"Wackawackawackawacka!"
>in the oakworlds, the leafnations,
>the dwelling places of the people
>with redfeathered heads,
>always joking and talking.

A squaw, maybe.
Yes. But one who doesn't yippiyi
when the braves ride back
waving scalps, who doesn't watch
the wardance, doesn't give a shit.

>Lice, squabbles, acorns.
>Always joking and talking.

Why do I keep thinking
about courage, about honor,
things I know nothing about?
But if honor, if they're wrong,
if honor is what's lost in battle?

                    The blackcapped chickadee
                    speaks a few times
                    clearly,
                    as if teaching a language.

O Arjuna!
if we used our hunger,
used our anger, otherwise?
Rilke the poet said "a *falling* happiness,"
and turned the world over for me.
Turning the world over in my hands
in tai chi turning
from right to left, from up to down,
I keep wondering about an honor
that might, with luck, if you knew how,
be like the new leaves of oak trees,
tender; about a valor
that would not withstand but run away
downhill, as easy as creek water.
If soul knew how to let itself be lost
as falling rain is lost,
what would be lost?

                    The hawk is back
                    to cry her hungry two notes
                    over the wild pastures
                    where the deermice
                    walk in their dwelling places.
                    The hawk is back
                    and angry.
                    She stoops to kill,
                    falls
                    like an arrow of bright rain.

As rain is lost
and runs away
into the world.

Well, it is so,
probably, almost certainly,
but I wish I could hear it
not only from woodpecker and chickadee,
see it not only in the barred wind-feather,
know it not only in the deermouse kiva,

but also in the words
and in the ways
and the dwelling places
of my own people.

IV

The Hill Yoncalla

From letters written about 1850 by Rozelle Applegate Putnam,
who was born in 1832 and came in the first
wagon train to Oregon in 1843.

I will try to do better next time

This is a real Oregon day
a slow warm rain is falling

My babe is a girl named Lucinda

I am in my father's house
where I have been all my life

You need not fear to undertake the trip

Last year a great many immigrants died of the cholera

Use no medicines on the road

Do not scruple to throw it away
let it be what it may

Yoncalla is not a town nor a place of man's creation
nor of a white man's naming
but it is a hill round and high and beautiful

I can get five pounds of dried peaches
for one pound of butter

the nearest neighbor three miles off

our little cabin quite a comfortable little place

A slow warm rain is falling
and will probably continue

I was called on to attend my mother
during her confinement
with her eleventh child

every branch and slough teeming then with salmon

Little Charley is very much like his father
the cats are his playmates
and he loves them dearly
Lucinda is just beginning to walk

All we have to wish for
is that you may all get here yet

A slow warm rain is falling
and will probably continue
a day and night without intermission

I will try to do better next time

From a letter of Jesse Applegate written in 1861

Rozelle after great suffering

eight little orphans added to our family

her short and humble life

All the words of this poem are taken from "The Letters of Roselle Putnam," edited by Sheba Hargreave, *Oregon Historical Quarterly* 24, no. 3 (1928).

A Traveler at a Lake in
New England

To take it in: as at the surface of the lake,
air and water meeting, there,
at the surface also of the air,
the water ceases being where
the air begins to be. So wholly is the body here.
Why not the spirit, entirely
resting on the air as water
and on the lake as air?

To do what happens to me, be
the size of my room, the lake,
the fuguing of the fireflies,
voices of strangers, sunset
remembered, and this other sea
from which the sun will strangely rise.

The Beach Runner

Clouds stand out over ocean
on pillars of falling rain.

The runner is kept from falling
by her own feet falling.

The lover is kept from sleeping
by her own heart aching.

After the falling, after the waking,
she learns to stand on pain.

Kate and Becca Housecleaning

Their bare feet step proud
as arch-necked horses.

Upstairs to downstairs
their voices call
like birds on high
and low branches.

Quick as sea winds
they blow through the house
and everything leaps, shakes,
and settles back peacefully shining.

In Berkeley

This is the city of my birth.
This is my own uneasy earth.
Following Time's devious laws,
I pass the stranger that I was.

In the sea-reflected light
that makes the shadows of things bright,
I walk a half-remembered street
and am the stranger that I meet.

Entanglements

March 28

Black cat, amiable visitor,
let's give each other
all the pleasure we can, quick,
yes, sitting on each other
in the sunlight and stroking
each other with our hands and faces,
being warm and tender and enjoyable,
yes, we should enjoy each other
while we are in the sun together
because all my black cats here
die and my friend here
dies by his own hand that lifts
and lifts the glass and the sunlight
doesn't last long here
with the land-wind blowing
and blowing tender and relentless
to the salt abyss, no place
for a cat or a friendship.

Night of March 28–29

Black cat don't twist my heart
around your crying
crouched at my door
with a dusty forehead, all night
crying and waiting for a person
who's no good to you.
Is a caress a promise?

Black cat I should be the one
making plans and you living wholly.
But you are making plans
without a future and my now
is twisted into your crying.

Yes sure I should have been able
to help somehow, I should be able
to help now somehow, something
more use than a pat on the shoulder
and Hi how's it going.

Is everything a promise?
Are all of them broken?

March 29

Black cat you are a fraud.
Your lady lives around the corner
and keeps her promises
or you wouldn't be the meaty
cat the hefty cat the bully cat
you are. A neighbor told me.
I should have listened to the crows
shouting Fraud! Fraud!
down from the phonepoles at you.
Pots calling the kettle.
You beat up his calico,
the neighbor said. Black hearted.
Bloody minded. A lesson to me.

Is everything a lesson?

Black is the lesson
I am learning from my friend.
How life gets twisted
until there's no way ever to untie it
because the future has become
the past and there is no now
no way. No way at all.

March 30

No way to love usefully.

March 31

Black cat you are a monster
wailing round the walls
and on the roof all night
crying and yowling let me in let me in
pet me pet me at three in the morning.
Caterwauling our modest affection
into a false inflated passion
a nonexistent drama of desertion
a little black misery. Oh why?
Why make us both miserable?
Why punish us? What for?
For sitting together in the sunlight?
What did we do wrong?

April 4

> Little demon of innocence,
> the sun's shining, let's caress
> again and sit on each other, yes,
> let's hurry, yes, to offer
> everything and count on nothing,
> make and break no promises
> and let no guilt
> and no experience
> come between the stroker and the stroked,
> the offer and the offering.
> Outside trust, what air
> is there to breathe?

The Stepmother

I could curse her.

Who is she with her grey hair
and wrinkles, hagridden,
powerless creature?
Why do I know her?

Ask me, says the mirror.
I reverse her.
She is careless, fearless,
fair, and she has power.

Old age

a new country. A different weather.
Different laws,
punitive, drastic, any infringement
punished at once by torture.
The language is common
only in ritual phrases
and silences.
The rest is dialects you don't understand.
Only sometimes on the bus
or in the waiting room
trying to figure out the forms,
somebody says a word that takes you
right back to the old country,
the big kitchen, everybody
talking at the same time,
everybody knowing everything together.

A Blue Moon: June 30

Cold north blows through hot sun.
I seek to be by doing things.
The wind does the wind; the sun is one;
I am the center of many rings,

a sphere enclosed in other spheres,
an absence in a solitude.
The sun is round, as round as years.
Is my hunger all my food?

A blue moon will rise tonight
as the sun sets across the wind.
I have done. I have done right.
Now let my being begin and sing.

The sun turns south; the wind is cold.
North and silence eat the old.

Aqueduct

For Keith

Words to say sorrow.
A line of bright days
each with a tomorrow
except this one.
Not my daughter. Not my son.
The water runs from the past
so fast, so clear.
The great arches
march across the years,
the mountains, the plains,
to bring the water
to the fountain
here.

Repulse Monkey

How I seek and seek through fear
a balance where I will be whole,
yet in scattered months of years
hide the fragments of my soul.

How I fear and fear to find
which is the year, the month, the week,
so that each movement of my mind
turns me away from what I seek,

that balance point, that backward chance,
the avoided center of the dance.

Calling

"Who's my little girl?" "Where is she?"
They'd call to me, Aunt Betsy and old May,
and I wouldn't answer, on the run.
Death knew what to call them. They laid aside
their stubborn selves like work
done, put their used hands away,
and leaving the houses they had kept,
answered to their names: Mary, Elizabeth.

"Will the Circle Be Unbroken?"

No, when they went, we said goodbye.

But why do we break through into love
to be instantly and constantly forsaken?
Is it a mere failure of perception
that makes the whole seem broken?

No, when I go, goodbye, I'm gone.

But still sometimes it seems like
the Grandmother Dance at the powwow,
the circling, the singing, and the endless drumming,
the intent faces passing, coming past, coming round.

Anon

Who is my mother,
the mother asks.
What do I call her?

I never knew her.
She was the sky
and the story teller.

I tell the stories
that I knew through her
but I cannot say her.

Who was my mother?
the mother asks.
No one can tell her.

Part Two

THE MIRROR
GALLERY

Only the names of the dead are true.
The others came
to me through the looking glass
as I walked in the lifelong gallery
looking and looking and asking them my name.

1. In the Summer Country

In the years before the war
among the friends and visitors
and refugees and anthropologists,
Stanislaw Klimek stayed with us a while
in the summer country.
The snapshot shows a man of thirty,
laughing, as he holds me on his shoulder.
Clearer than the camera I remember
the first sweet opening promise,
the handsome man
flattered and tender to the child
who fell in love with him
right then at the beginning and for good.

I have seen him since: the Polish Rider
that maybe Rembrandt painted,
hand on hip and turning straight
out of the painting
his radiant, kind, proud face.
Klimek went back to his country;
a scholar, a cavalry officer,
mounted and spurred his horse
against the machine guns
of 1939. Probably.
There is no way to know.
The names were lost,
the corpses bulldozed
into the ground. My father said:
I hope he was killed
then, at the beginning.

Only the names of the dead are true.

2. Phebe and Mimi

Into the co-op paper sack
I can measure rice by eye
just to top the canister at home.
Not for nothing a grocer's granddaughter.

A silent bell
trembles in the even dark
of dead of winter morning
at six-fifteen, to wake
the clockmaker's granddaughter.

But what of her who rode the stallion
men could not bridle,
what am I, pedestrian, of her?
An implacable memory
of her cut-glass goblets.

Of the other I have
a fringed black silken shawl,
a few letters in the old script of German
written to her son my father.

Wives of bankrupts
(the grocery failed, the clockshop failed)
who came West,
(the New World, the Rocky Mountains)
they kept the house and the accounts,

bore and brought up sons and daughters.
I cry to them, I cannot read you!
You are unmeasured, left out of time!

Not for nothing were they housewives.

Look at the two photographs:
mouths closed,
lip to firm lip.
Contained. Containing.

3. The Great Aunt

She had her smell.
Lamb and ewe know ewe and lamb
among the hundreds.
This one and no one else!
I nuzzled into Betsy.

She told me the story:
They got the horses out of the burning barn,
hitched up and drove away
while the house burned down behind them.
Nothing left to stay for.
But the pump in the wellhouse
that always kept beating
like the heart of the ranch
was still beating and beating
and the child in the wagon
kept the fire burning and the heart beating
as they drove away across Wyoming.

Why did she marry Uncle Charlie?
They all wondered.
Could have had her pick
and picked the shiftless.
She never told that story.

She wore a brooch
that pressed a mark between
her deep breasts.
She held her cigarette
between two upright fingers.

"After my sister died," she said,
"my writing changed.
I used to write a fine Spencerian.
After she died I tried to write
and did not recognize my hand."
She said, "My mother
did not want me. My sister Phebe,
twenty when I was born,
she was my mother.
Sister Ann, Sister Ann!" she said,
smiling, when she thought of Phebe:
"*Sister Ann, is anybody coming?*
I used to call her Sister Ann.
I never loved anyone
as I loved her."

Betsy had traveled all around the West
with a little humpback trunk,
The Count of Monte Cristo,
and a complete set of Dickens.
Knowing a good deal about mules and horses,
she was critical of movie cowboys,
except for Gary Cooper.
"The man can ride," she said.

There were six brothers
between her and Phebe.
Homer and Lafayette had been blown up
on a train platform in the mine troubles.
To me it was a silent film,

board sidewalks, wood-burning engines,
silver mines. I did not have brothers
who were destroyed.

She lived with us till I was ten
and I was two mothers' daughter.
I knew she loved my brother
better than me and didn't care.
What's better than water?

She spoke of a woman who disliked her.
I was indignant—How could she?
"Well," said Betsy,
"I pity her poor taste."

Another story: was it a brother
or the badluck husband
who found the opal mine?
Prospecting the Nevada, Utah, somewhere
in the desert, built a campfire in a ring of rocks,
and pam! a rock burst open!
and the core of opal shining in the flames!
Marked the place as best he could,
took what he could, but they were boulders
too heavy for the mule, headed for town,
got lost, found the road finally,
but never could get back,
never found the way again
to where the opals were
hidden in the hearts of rocks.

I have the little brooch she wore.
It's only glass,
the jeweler told me. Fire opal,
she said and we believed. Fire opal!
In her voice
all the desert and the dream
and the lost way
from the fire burning
far back across the distance of the years.

4. Friends of My Youth

The Parade

How grotesque, how wonderful
the parade of the visiting grown-ups!

Stiff upright little Giff, announced, encircled
by the smell of his cigars,
even stronger than his character; his wife Delilah
like a flowery sofa, soft and open-armed,
childlike, childless.

Cy taught me penmanship and swimming
by strange methods of her own devising,
wore footless stockings on her arms
because of embolisms,
rasped, bossed, bullied,
taught, talked, ticced:
a cartload of New England gravel
wed strangely to the Viennese Professor,
convex, distinguished, bland,
secretive,
in whose world there were no children.

Angular, erratic as a building-crane,
dry-voiced, Mary Ellen was dying slowly
of the cortisone they gave her for arthritis,
but every year
she and her accountant husband
still took a few hundred dollars to Reno
and gambled every cent away
and came back happy

to their treehouse in the Berkeley hills
facing the sunset.

The famous child psychologist,
my mother's friend from college,
arrived to stay her week with us
with gorgeous bakery cakes, boxes of pastries,
candy, all the stuff we never got.
She'd flop them down in the kitchen,
flop herself down in a bedroom,
sleep for a night and a day and a night
and wake up—I've had my rest for this year!—
and talk and smoke a cigarette down one inch
and put it out and light the next and talk and laugh,
mild, formidable, anybody's equal,
a childless woman whose mind was full of children.

At the Irrigation Tank

How amazing they were in bathing suits!
The hairs, the veins, the bulges,
the bluewhite thighs, the gnarly feet,
how interesting, compared to us,
sleek skinny fish, unfinished,
all pretty, all the same.

They never stayed in long
and never swam underwater.

There was the Veteran who coughed.
He had been gassed. There was the Priest
in bathing trunks, legs columnar,
forearms and chest all stiff gray curls,
the only priest I knew,

half-naked. There was the Cousin
who spat, the way men used to spit,
out of pure manliness, even from the pool,
raising up to clear the edge.
And there was May,
blue wires of varicose, ninety in a bathing suit
with little flowers on it,
kicking the bluestoned water bright
in the dry blaze of July
as she sat on the rough edge of the tank
to gossip with Betsy and my mother.

None of them ever
swam underwater.
They were the airbreathers.
We still had gills.

5. The Fight

Constance was my enemy.
I have no idea why.
Constance, if you are alive,
do you remember why we fought,
tooth and nail, fist and foot,
right down on the rough asphalt
in a circle of fascinated girls?
The boys paid no attention.
Girls fight dirty,
biting, kicking, scratching, pulling hair.
So what's long hair for?
What's hate for?
Boys fight fair. Men fight
just wars. We fought
in hate and then forgot.
The bell rang for the end of recess,
and we quit.
My ancient and my constant enemy,
what was it about?

6. T

Three of us
under the loquat bush
in that earthy twisty leafy room,
very low-ceilinged,
shot through with sunlight.
Nine, ten, twelve.
Girl, boy, boy.
Let's play T.

Two were the torturers.
Turns were taken.
Tickling, mostly,
elaborate immobilizations,
exquisite tensions,
terrors and giggling.
I want to be It now!

Fritz, my friend,
was the best victim,
helpless with laughter
as soon as we touched him.
I and my brother,
imaginative,
devised surprises.
A blindfold. A leaf drawn
slowly, slowly

from back of knee to instep.
Fritz stifled luxurious screams.

There was a reason
for only playing T
under the secret loquat
and for not letting the laughter
and the screams be heard.
Adults would not
have understood
what we were doing.

7. Skating

When we were eleven my friend Paula
and I went skating
at the ice rink.
Paula was pretty good. She said,
"You look like a monkey in red pants."
I said, "What?"
She said, "There's a girl here
in red pants, but not you,
and she looks like a fat monkey
and she can't skate."
I said, "Where?"
"Oh, skating around," said Paula
and skated off.

We didn't play at her house
because of her mother yelling.
When we were playing at my house
Paula would get mad at me
for no reason at all, and cry.

8. First

I truly don't remember what his name was
or anything about the boy.
We sat on the little stone seat
on the landing of the long stone steps
that led to my high house
in the dim streetlight of 1944
and kissed each other on the lips
and then got sort of stuck
in the stiff embrace.
I heard his wristwatch ticking by my ear
and said, "Your watch is ticking,"
and he murmured, "What?"
and I said, "Your watch is ticking."
Somehow we detached. We climbed the rest
of the long stone steps to the front door
and said good night
tenderly, politely, with relief.
I went inside and went to bed
and lay in the cool sweet wind of night
that brought in through the open window
the solemn Campanile chime,
and thought, "My first kiss," solemnly.
And indeed it is a solemn thing.
I hope he too remembers it
and has forgotten me.

9. The Hershey Bar

Oh how I loved the man!
Fair, slight, thirtyish,
handkerchief tucked in his sleeve
like Lord Peter Wimsey. He was
a little weary and a little dry.
He was in uniform.
My whole soul was the bow,
he the unknowing violin.
I drew a music from that man
he never heard. A crush
was the technical name for it,
that pure tune,
that morning robin raga.
He silenced it by bringing me
a half-pound Hershey bar.
Only soldiers could get chocolate like that.
A thoughtful present
for his friends' fourteen-year-old.
I took the leaden bar
and muttered Thank you
(a quick glance from my mother,
what's amiss?)
I took it to my room
and ate it
slowly, square after square,
silent, not sharing.
A food not of love nor music.
Solid nourishment
for a growing girl.

10. Tony

The biggest friend I ever had was Tony.
For a wormy apple
he'd let me clamber from the gate
onto his vast back
in the sweet smell of horse sweat
and ride him, hours, rambling
the dry wild pastures
of the summer hills,
nobody else in the grasshopper-singing world.
He grazed, I dreamed,
rocking like a boat in sunlight.
At last he'd remember he was out to pasture,
drift under a low-branched live oak
and scrape me off as easy
as butter off a plate.
So I'd give him the last apple
and go home
over the hills of fourteen summers
bowlegged,
singing like a grasshopper.

11. Susannah

She was beautiful,
my friend Susannah.
Fair, thin, tall, grey-eyed,
kind of wild but very gentle,
like the wild lilies
of the Big Sur country,
those high headlands
in the fog above the ocean.
    We met when we were ten
at a Halloween party.
She was a Black Panther.
Thin little face like a candle flame
under the black cat ears.
    Her aunt Polly wanted us to be friends.
I always bossed her,
but she was the brave one.
She went for the ladder
and didn't laugh at me
stuck in a panic five feet up
in the tree she could climb to the top of.
    Once she told Jean and me:
when she lived with her father and mother
way back in the Big Sur country,
somebody gave them a whole ham.
They were so happy.
They'd eat for a week!
When they cut it
there were worms all through it
thick as fingers.
They threw it out
and her father cried.
    She didn't have a father

when I knew her.
          She moved to a different city
and got more beautiful.
          I went off to college.
She got married
and had a baby, got divorced,
remarried, had a baby, got divorced,
married again and had another baby,
while I was still East
being educated.
          When I came back West I asked Jean,
"Who's Susannah married to now,
the movie guy or the rich guy
or the prizewinning writer, or who?"
          "You don't know?" Jean said.
"Well, she divorced the writer.
She was living with the kids
down there in the Big Sur country.
She was driving home from her job
in the dark, in the fog,
and the car went off the road."
          I started to say something.
"No!" Jean said.
"She had three kids
and she was taking care of them
and working. Anybody
can go off those roads
in the dark, in the fog,
above the ocean."

12. Jean

If I say friend it is her name.

Sixteen years dead, and vivid
as the storm that shakes this house this day,
the April light, the white narcissus.

I hated her. She stole
plump Margaret from me.
She flaunted her red head and freckled arms
and laughed aloud. So I went after her.
Too bad for Margaret and loyalty.
I won. I won the race. I won the prize
for life. Both lives.
            Hours, hours on the telephone.
Waiting for the morning bus to come
down Euclid with her on it,
the fox-red hair, the milky skin,
the grin. She had a wit
like a blade of flame. Reality
was her cookie. She swam
in truth like a salmon in the river.
            She cheated on a history test
in tenth grade, and got caught.
She would. She stood
fire-red with shame.
            Eighteen, and sitting underneath a bush
in a huge garden at a huge wedding
in Shaker Heights in Cleveland,
me and Jean and her uncle John
and a bottle of champagne,
hiding from the wedding guests
who were all talking about Jackie Robinson

and next thing you know they'll be living
next door here.
"I don't know what to be!"
sang Jean like a robin redbreast.
Her Uncle John the novelist
said, "Be a courtesan.
The life is easy and the money's good."
We finished off the bottle of champagne.

She was a secretary. No. That isn't
what she was. She was a wife
and mother. Yes. But that isn't
what she was. She was
the refiner's fire.

Once I saw a movie of
that tall red racehorse, Man o' War,
running unridden through a field of grass,
gallant, generous, playful, free.
Can fire be kind?

She died of cancer. No,
I want to say, that isn't
true. She was forty-six. No,
I want to say. I want the years
I seldom saw her, when she hauled
the trash of other people's lives
like any cart-horse woman. And I want
myself to have been brave.
To have been equal to her honesty.

The last time I saw her
she was bald.
The wig dummy stood on the chest of drawers,

featureless white styrofoam.
"I hate that," she said. "I hate it."
Her daughter and I stuck eye-buttons on it,
lipsticked it, made it a funny face.
It was more horrible.
        All I could ask of all I might have asked
was, "Are you scared?"
and Jean said, "I wish the kids
were a little older. It would be easier
for them."

A red fire burning.
A white narcissus.
A tiny ivory egg
we bought in Chinatown
and traded back and forth for years.
After she died
I couldn't find it.

13. College

When I was in college
one of the graduate students
was my instructor in the course
in what a woman is
to be. And the vocabulary.
Soon I spoke only in four letters,
the language of our love.
He taught me how to lie
both down and to,
and I was a straight A student.
Next he started teaching me
why women have abortions.
I wanted to drop that course.
Hey, I said, look,
let me teach you
trust. It's really easy.
I have so much of it
you don't even have to learn it,
I can just give it to you.
But he taught me
that he didn't need anything I had,
because he had tenure
at a very old, exclusive college.
So I learned my lesson.
And I paid the tuition.
And I was graduated
without honors.

14. Angel

When I was twenty-one I had a friend
who left his angel in New York.
A ten-cent Woolworth's plastic angel, white,
with a gold halo and a secret smile.
She looked like somebody
he used to know, he said.
He left her on the table by the bed
in his hotel room.
He telegraphed me from his ship,
halfway to Paris.
I went, and the hotel clerk grinned
and gave me the angel.
She stood on the table by my bed
all summer, smiling
at the sweet California mornings,
and I wrote poems in French
to the man who lost his angel,
but didn't send them.
Come September the ship went west,
the train went east,
and in New York
I gave my friend his angel.
He gave me a bottle of perfume from Paris.
It spilled in the bureau
of my dormitory room,
every drop, gone.
A faint smell of angel
on everything I wore
for a week or so.

15. Graduate School

Ellen brought a faun with her
from Arkansas
to graduate school. She drew him once:
the curling mouth, the liquid eye,
the horn buds,
and pinned him up on the wall of her room.
   Her friend Lorena,
schoolteacher in her forties,
a little lamed by polio,
witty, sensible, midwestern,
cowered in Ellen's room, shuddering,
the night the undergraduate men
held a panty raid,
storming the graduate women's dorm.
   I was incredulous of her terror.
"They're just dumb boys,
they aren't going to *do* anything!"
   They chanted in the courtyard,
scrambled to windowsills,
howled in the hallways.
Bright-eyed with fury,
Ellen held Lorena in her arms,
murmuring, "It will be all right.
It will be all right."

Inscrutable
the faun she drew
looked down on us.

16. Bella

I longed to know her
but she drifted off
elusive into bright mists
of laughter, and I couldn't follow.

I didn't know for years
that the mist was vodka
and she had nowhere to go
and nobody knew her.

17. Caravel

In a foreign land
I had a friend
who was very tall,
like a sailing ship
leaning a little forward.
Her laugh cracked like a pennant.
Teacups in her large hands
looked tiny as toys,
but the tea
was fragrant and plentiful,
sweetened with beautiful brown crystals
brought from the Indies.
The long flags snapped
and my friend leaned forward
talking, all sails set
to the trade winds sweeping forever
round the wide, warm world.

They tell me that she is beset,
fast in the ice,
immobile, listing a little
in the dark wind
at the sea's end.

18. Family

She is a nice woman
and loves her children
and sends an annual
xerox letter to her friends
about them. Timothy
took his degree with highest honors,
Donald won
the All-State Writing Competition,
and Rosemary at fifteen
has organized a program
of skiing lessons for inner-city children.
At another Christmas,
Timothy owns General Electronics,
Donald has won the Pulitzer,
and Rosemary the Nobel Peace Prize.
It is a proud moment for the family.
And the awful thing is,
it is true.
Every word of it.

19. Player

Once I had this actor friend
who was into chemicals.
His mind was all different
colors. Like a crazy quilt
coming to pieces.
There were the blue pieces
like soft velvet, and the bright
print bits, and the patches
of gorgeous crimson satin,
and the torn silks, and the holes
getting bigger.
When the winter came
he had nothing for cover
but his crazy quilt,
all torn to rags
because he kept stumbling on the edges
when he wore it as a cloak
on the stage, where he played God.
He didn't know
how to sew, he only knew
one kind of needle.
My friend died
of exposure
in a dark theater.

20. Religious Connections

She wasn't my doctor's regular nurse.
She listened to my murmuring heart
stutter its congenital wrong word,
listened to the other little heart
babbling below it, and said, "Pray.
It's all you can do, dear.
Just pray, pray, pray!
Doctor will be in in a minute."
And she brisked out, plump with Jesus.

That was thirty years ago,
but in my mind I've married her
to the man who stands outside the clinic
screaming at the girls going in.
And they make quite a couple.

21. The Flower Painter

He could purr like a cat,
but didn't like cats.
Loved his dog. Her first litter,
she had thirteen puppies.
His wives lost count
of their pregnancies,
abortions, stillbirths, babies.
He wouldn't hurt a fly.
Never bathed or used a condom,
protecting little lives,
sperm, bacteria. Marriage
came so easy to him.
"Why do they divorce me?"
He sickened at the smell of meat.

22. Circles

The child runs
and runs
in circles
silently,
lips tight,
striking with his fists
at chairs, people,
the air:
as if one of the unnumbered
children starved, defiled,
murdered
by the brutal fathers
of power and of war
had been reborn in him to live
and rage
and rage
and rage,
but speechless.
His gentle father
and his gentle mother speak
of what can
and cannot be done.

23. Joy

And now the letter comes:
the ice breaks, the caravel drifts free
across the ocean of the night.
And I can say her name.

Maybe now the word
she carved in a great curve of wood
like the hollow of a flower
or a trumpet's flare or a wind-filled sail
is her true name.

24. At Oakley

I was out there last week at Oakley
forty-five years later.
Huge walled estates of houses
surround the little town
near the Sacramento where it widens to the Bay.
I couldn't find Betsy's house, or the walnut trees
that made the arching, starry darkness where I
    walked
with Lee, my cousin once removed,
talking for the first time with a grown-up man
about life and love. Lee said
not to worry, I'd find love all right.
If I didn't in five years,
and he'd tried marrying twice
and it hadn't worked out, well then,
we could get married, him and me.
We laughed, we shook hands on it. For years
I treasured that, I held that comfort,
that kind man, in my heart.
Nothing worked out very well for Lee.
He died in his forties. The orchards
of high walnut trees are gone,
paved with bedrooms. The road's still there
where I walked with Lee's mother,
Betsy, when I stayed with her
at the little house in Oakley.
The big trucks roared along that road
stinking and shaking the warm evenings of the Delta.
"I always think," she said,
"when they go by like that,
that's Death just missed me."

25. The Door

I am to find the face, they say,
I had before I was born.
Shall I look for it in her
who bore me?

"The Baby Lake," my father said, Victorian,
Freudian, teasing, with a grin.
Little faces floating in the Baby Lake
like water-lilies, looking up.
Mine isn't there.

Who was she before?
How shall I know her
or who it is I seek
in what high waters above earth,
above thin air?

The mother is the door
but not the mirror.
My mother's daughter and my daughters' mother,
still I look, look for her.

26. You, Her, I

Oh but I cannot give you up.
Oh but I cannot twist away
among the mirrors of the words
the corridors reflecting corridors
and never come
and never come to you.

Oh but I cannot come to you.

When I was a child
I'd build a labyrinth of blocks
and move a little mirror through it
and look in that and so be in the labyrinth,
seeing only the empty corridor ahead.
So I explored the mystery I made.

Sometimes there is a fountain in the center.
Sometimes a monster.

Galleries reflecting galleries.

Sometimes there is no center.

Shall I evade you all my life
and call it looking for you?
Words would never hold you.
To whom does an old woman say
Mother, let me come to you?

You never lied
but your truth was myth.
Men all adored you.

The sun, the changing moon.
You wriggled out of your girdle.
You liked to let your stockings,
unfastened from their garters, droop,
while you walked around undressing.
Turquoise and heavy silver
on your wrists and fingers.

Your first husband gave you
two sons and early sorrow.
Your second gave you
a son and me and migraines and Peru
and I think your power.
Your third gave you the isle of Avalon.
Oh but I go around the corner
and meet the reflected corner
and there is no one
in the corridors.

When her back ached I helped put
the mustard plaster on the soft, soft
freckled skin, and later peeled it off
from the fiery shoulders. Tell me if it hurts.
That's all right, go on.

I wonder when I hurt her most.
It never occurred to me I could.
How power denies itself!

All the letters back and forth,
the easy conversations
in the kitchen, stuff of life,

strong lovely fabric, torn
and stained, unwearable.

Are you where I must toil to come
so that I can go on at all,
or sun, moon, valley
of my going?
Lost key or open door?

That you died in fear and pain
is fear and pain and that you lived
is life to me. Your freedom
is my standing ground. You said,
"When I am dead, forget me."
Fat chance! and you knew it.

How can I come to you
who never left?
Bereft, ungrateful, I must turn away
to make the mythic distance true.